THE HEALTHY KITCHEN

PALEO

hinkler

CONTENTS

Introduction 3

Breakfast 5

Lunch 23

Dinner 41

Dessert 59

Drinks 77

Weights and Measures 94

Index 96

hinkler

Published by Hinkler Books Pty Ltd
45–55 Fairchild Street
Heatherton Victoria 3202 Australia
www.hinkler.com.au

Design © Hinkler Books Pty Ltd 2015
Food photography and recipe development
© Stockfood, The Food Media Agency
Typesetting: MPS Limited
Prepress: Graphic Print Group

ISBN: 978 1 7436 7731 5

Printed and bound in China

PALEO

The Paleo diet has become well known thanks to Dr Loren Cordain, PhD, the founder of the Paleo movement. The diet is based on the theory that to keep fit and healthy we should eat the natural foods that our ancestors would have eaten during the Paleolithic (Stone Age) era, around ten thousand years ago.

In his book *The Paleo Diet: Lose Weight and Get Healthy by Eating the Foods You Were Designed to Eat* (Houghton Mifflin Harcourt; Revised edition 3 Dec 2010), Dr Cordain maintains that processed foods have had a disastrous effect on our health, giving rise to modern illnesses, such as cancer, type 2 diabetes, heart disease and obesity. The Paelo diet is high in valuable nutrients and has been found to stabilise blood sugar levels, increase energy and promote a strong immune system.

Dr Cordain and his team found that following the Paleo diet helps you lose weight, reduce the risk of cardiovascular disease, lower blood pressure and reduce acne.

This book contains a huge range of recipes to help you plan nutritious meals while following a Paleo diet. The diet includes free-range meat; poultry; game; offal (organ meats); seafood; eggs; mushrooms; nuts; seeds; herbs; spices; unrefined vegetable, plant and seed oils; fresh fruits and vegetables; water and herbal teas. When buying foods for the diet, it's important to buy the best quality ingredients, such as grass-fed beef, wild fish (as opposed to farmed), free-range eggs, sea salt and good-quality unrefined oils, such as olive and coconut oil.

Foods to avoid on the Paleo diet include dairy foods, cereals, pulses (legumes), refined sugar and salt, processed foods, starchy vegetables and alcohol. However, some followers of the diet do include some legumes and grains, such as peas and corn, as these can be eaten freshly picked and raw. Some followers also include some starchy vegetables – such as sweet potatoes – to provide carbohydrates, which are needed for energy. In order to make for a more well-rounded and healthy diet, there are also a few starchy vegetables in our recipes.

If you're looking to lose weight, there's no weighing, measuring or counting calories on the Paleo diet – you eat until you feel satisfied.

BREAKFAST

For a refreshing start to the day, choose a breakfast that doesn't come out of a box. These creative recipes use Paleo ingredients that will help sustain your energy throughout the day.

PANCAKES WITH BANANAS

Serves 4
Preparation and cooking 25 minutes

Ingredients:

4 eggs
225 ml | 8 fl oz | 1 cup coconut milk
1 tbsp maple syrup
55 g | 2 oz | ½ cup coconut flour
1 tsp bicarbonate of (baking) soda
¼ tsp salt
1 firm banana, sliced
light olive oil, for cooking

To serve:
maple syrup
lemon wedges

Method:

1. Whisk the eggs until frothy, then whisk in the coconut milk and maple syrup until smooth.

2. Sift in the coconut flour, bicarbonate of (baking) soda and salt and beat well to a thick batter. Stir in the banana.

3. Heat a little oil in a frying pan (skillet) and cook large spoonfuls of the batter in batches for 3–4 minutes on each side, until golden brown.

4. Serve warm with maple syrup and lemon wedges.

CARROT AND CINNAMON MUFFINS

Makes 12 muffins
Preparation and cooking 50 minutes

Ingredients:

300 g | 11 oz | 2 cups very finely ground almonds
½ tsp sea salt
1 tsp bicarbonate of (baking) soda
2 tsp ground cinnamon
40 g | 1½ oz | ½ cup desiccated (fine) coconut
110 ml | 4 fl oz | 7 tbsp melted coconut oil
3 eggs
150 g | 5 oz | 7 tbsp honey
1 large carrot, grated
50 g | 1¾ oz | ½ cup chopped pistachio nuts

Method:

1. Heat the oven to 180°C (160°C fan | 350°F | gas 4). Place paper cases in a 12-hole muffin tin.

2. Combine the almonds, salt, bicarbonate of (baking) soda, cinnamon and coconut in a mixing bowl.

3. Stir together the oil, eggs, honey and grated carrots and stir into the dry ingredients until just combined then gently stir in the chopped pistachios.

4. Spoon the mixture into the paper cases and bake for 25–30 minutes or until firm to the touch. Cool in the tin for 5 minutes, then place on a wire rack to cool completely.

VEGETABLE FRITTATAS

Serves 4
Preparation and cooking 30 minutes

Ingredients:

6 tbsp sunflower oil
150 g | 5 oz | 2 cups sliced mushrooms
3 medium zucchinis (courgettes), grated
4 spring (green) onions, chopped
4 eggs, lightly beaten
2 tsp sea salt

Method:

1. Heat two tablespoons of the oil in a large frying pan (skillet) and gently cook the mushrooms until they are soft and starting to brown. Remove the mushrooms from the pan and wipe it clean with kitchen paper.

2. Heat another two tablespoons of oil and cook the zucchinis (courgettes) until tender. Remove the zucchinis from the pan and wipe it clean again.

3. Mix the mushrooms, zucchinis and spring (green) onions into the beaten eggs and season with salt.

4. Heat the remaining oil in the pan, pour in the vegetable mixture and cook over a gentle heat until the eggs are set. Remove the pan from the heat and let the frittata cool a little before sliding it onto a serving plate. Serve warm or cold.

FRITTERS WITH MUSHROOM SAUCE

Serves 4
Preparation and cooking 25 minutes

Ingredients:

3 zucchinis (courgettes), coarsely grated
1 onion, grated
3 eggs, beaten
1 tbsp coconut flour
salt
freshly ground black pepper
vegetable oil, for frying

For the mushroom sauce:
1 tbsp olive oil
200 g | 7 oz mushrooms, sliced
1–2 garlic cloves, crushed
3 tbsp coconut milk
120 ml | 4 fl oz | ½ cup chicken stock (broth)
sea salt and pepper
1 tbsp parsley

To garnish:
dill (dill weed) or onion flowers

Method:

1. Dry the zucchinis (courgettes) in a tea towel, then mix with the onion in a bowl.

2. Beat the eggs and sift in the coconut flour and beat again. Stir into the zucchini mixture. Season with salt and pepper to taste.

3. Heat the oil in a large frying pan (skillet) over a medium heat. Drop large tablespoons of the mixture in the pan and cook for 2–3 minutes on each side until crisp and golden brown.

4. Drain on absorbent kitchen paper.

5. For the mushroom sauce: heat the oil in the frying pan. Add the mushrooms and garlic and sauté until browned.

6. Add the coconut milk and chicken stock (broth) and stir. Bring to the boil and then reduce heat and simmer until the sauce thickens.

7. Season with salt and pepper and stir in parsley. Place in a separate dish to serve.

8. Garnish fritters with dill (dill weed) or onion flowers and serve with mushroom sauce.

NUT AND SEED BREAKFAST

Serves 4–6
Preparation and cooking 30 minutes

Ingredients:

150 g | 5 oz | 2 cups sliced almonds
75 g | 2½ oz | 1 cup flaked coconut
70 g | 2½ oz | ½ cup sesame seeds
120 g | 4 oz | 1 cup sunflower seeds
135 g | 5 oz | 1 cup pumpkin seeds
55 ml | 2 fl oz | 11 tsp maple syrup
75 ml | 2½ fl oz | ⅓ cup coconut oil

Method:

1. Heat the oven to 170°C (150°C fan | 335°F | gas 3). Line a large baking tray (sheet) with non-stick baking paper.

2. Mix together the almonds, coconut and seeds.

3. Heat the maple syrup and coconut oil until just melted. Stir into the nuts and seeds to coat.

4. Spread evenly on the baking tray and bake for about 20 minutes until golden brown. Cool completely on the baking tray, then break into pieces to serve.

BELGIAN WAFFLES

Serves 4
Preparation and cooking 40 minutes

Ingredients:

3 eggs, separated
55 ml | 2 fl oz | 11 tsp coconut milk
150 g | 5 oz | 1 cup very finely ground almonds
¼ tsp sea salt
1 tsp vanilla extract
1 tbsp maple syrup, plus extra to serve
2 tbsp coconut oil, melted
fresh berries, to serve

Method:

1. Heat a waffle iron and grease lightly.

2. Beat the egg yolks with the coconut milk in a large bowl until the mixture is light and fluffy.

3. Add the almonds and salt and mix until smooth, then stir in the vanilla, maple syrup and melted coconut oil.

4. Whisk the egg whites until stiff then gradually fold them into the almond batter.

5. Make the waffles in the waffle iron according to the manufacturer's instructions until cooked through and golden brown. Repeat until all the batter is used.

6. Serve the waffles in stacks topped with maple syrup and berries.

ALMOND AND CARROT BREAD

Makes 1 loaf
Preparation and cooking 50 minutes

Ingredients:

250 g | 9 oz | 2 cups almond flour
150 g | 5 oz | 1 cup chopped almonds
2 large carrots, finely grated
1 tsp salt
½ tsp bicarbonate of (baking) soda
2 eggs, lightly beaten
1 tsp honey
1 tsp lemon juice

Method:

1. Heat the oven to 180°C (160°C fan | 350°F | gas 4).

2. Mix the almond flour, chopped almonds, carrots, salt and bicarbonate of (baking) soda in a large bowl.

3. Mix together the eggs, honey and lemon juice then add to the dry ingredients. Work the mixture into a stiff dough, adding a little cold water if necessary, and form it into a loaf shape.

4. Place the loaf in a greased tin or baking tray (sheet) and bake in the oven for 30–40 minutes. Let the loaf cool before you slice it.

FLUFFY BAKED EGGS WITH ROASTED-VEGETABLE HASH

Serves 4
Preparation and cooking 40 minutes

Ingredients:

4 eggs, separated
salt
freshly ground pepper

For the vegetable hash:
150 g | 5 oz mushrooms, chopped
1 sweet potato (yam), diced
2 shallots, thinly sliced
3 tbsp olive oil
½ tsp salt
freshly ground black pepper

Method:

1. Heat the oven to 200°C (180°C fan | 400°F | gas 6). Grease 4 ramekins or small baking dishes.

2. Whisk the egg whites until stiff, but not dry.

3. Lightly whisk the egg yolks in a separate bowl. Add ¼ of the egg whites to the egg yolks and whisk gently to combine. Season to taste with salt and pepper.

4. Gently fold in the remaining egg whites.

5. Divide between the ramekins and bake for 10–15 minutes, until cooked to your liking.

6. For the vegetable hash: toss together the mushrooms, sweet potato (yam), shallots, oil, salt and pepper and put into a baking dish in an even layer.

7. Bake for about 15 minutes until tender and golden brown.

8. Serve the eggs immediately, topped with the roasted vegetables.

LUNCH

These healthy lunch recipes are a great way to increase your vegetable intake. Many also include a source of protein. There are hearty lunches for the cooler months, lighter lunches for the warmer months and options that work well all year round.

CHILLI CHICKEN WRAPS

Makes 4 wraps
Preparation and cooking 40 minutes + 1 hour marinating

Ingredients:

1 green chilli, seeds removed, finely chopped
2 tbsp honey
3 tbsp lime juice
2½ cm | 1" piece ginger (gingerroot), grated
1 tsp paprika
1 tsp salt
½ tsp freshly ground black pepper
8 chicken drumsticks

To serve:
lettuce leaves
avocado slices
cherry tomatoes, halved
radishes
sliced red onion

To garnish:
coriander (cilantro)
lime wedges

Method:

1. Whisk together the first 7 ingredients.

2. Slash the drumsticks with a sharp knife and put into a shallow non-metallic dish and pour over the marinade. Cover and marinate at room temperature for at least 1 hour, turning occasionally.

3. Heat the oven to 190°C (170°C fan | 375°F | gas 5).

4. Place the drumsticks in a shallow baking dish, shaking off any excess marinade. Cook for about 20 minutes, until the chicken is cooked through with no trace of pink juices when pierced with a knife. Pour over the remaining marinade and cook for 5 minutes, until sticky and browned.

5. Lay out the lettuce leaves, overlapping to form a wrap. Arrange the chicken and vegetables on the lettuce and garnish with coriander (cilantro) and lime wedges.

SPICY SWEET-POTATO SOUP

Serves 4
Preparation and cooking 50 minutes

Ingredients:

2 tbsp olive oil
1 onion, finely chopped
1–2 cloves garlic, crushed
6 sweet potatoes (yams), diced
1 red capsicum (pepper), seeds removed, diced
1 yellow capsicum (pepper), seeds removed, diced
1 red chilli, seeds removed, diced
1 l | 35 fl oz | 4 cups vegetable stock (broth)
½ tsp paprika
salt and pepper, to taste
grated nutmeg, to taste

To garnish:
coconut flakes
coriander seeds, coarsely crushed

Method:

1. Heat the oil in a large pan and cook the onions until starting to soften.

2. Add the garlic and cook for a further 2–3 minutes.

3. Add the sweet potatoes (yams), capsicums (peppers) and chilli and cook for a further 10 minutes, stirring occasionally.

4. Stir in the stock (broth) and paprika, cover and simmer very gently for about 20 minutes, until the sweet potato is tender. Cool slightly.

5. Transfer ⅓–½ the soup to a blender or food processor and blend until smooth.

6. Return to the pan and season to taste with salt, pepper and nutmeg. Reheat gently and serve garnished with flaked coconut and coriander seeds.

Tip: Croutons are not acceptable on a Paleo diet unless made from special Paleo grain-free bread.

MUSSELS IN CURRY BROTH

Serves 4
Preparation and cooking 30 minutes

Ingredients:

2 tbsp olive oil
2 shallots, finely chopped
1 clove garlic, finely chopped
2 tbsp curry paste or powder
400 ml | 14 fl oz | 1⅔ cups coconut milk
330 ml | 12 fl oz | 1⅓ cups vegetable stock (broth)
3 tbsp lemon juice
2 bay leaves
1 kg | 2¼ lb mussels, scrubbed, beards removed

To garnish:
chopped parsley

Method:

1. Heat the oil in a large heavy-based pan. Add the shallots, garlic and curry paste or powder and cook, stirring for about 1 minute until fragrant.

2. Add the coconut milk, stock (broth), lemon juice and bay leaves and bring to a simmer. Simmer for 10 minutes.

3. Add the mussels. Increase the heat, cover the pan, bring to a boil and cook for 4–8 minutes until all the mussels are open. Discard any mussels that don't open.

4. Place the mussels in a serving bowl. Boil the sauce until slightly thickened, stirring occasionally. Season with salt and pepper and discard the bay leaves.

5. Spoon the sauce over the mussels and sprinkle with parsley.

SMOKED DUCK SALAD

Serves 4
Preparation and cooking 15 minutes

Ingredients:

120 g | 4 oz smoked duck slices
2 heads chicory (endive), leaves separated
100 g | 3½ oz rocket (arugula)
70 g | 2½ oz baby spinach
1–2 pomegranates, seeds only
3 tbsp walnut oil
3 tbsp extra virgin olive oil
2 tbsp pomegranate molasses
1 tbsp red wine vinegar
4–5 tbsp toasted flaked almonds
coarsely crushed black peppercorns

Method:

1. Divide the duck, chicory leaves, rocket (arugula) and baby spinach among 4 serving plates, then scatter with the pomegranate seeds.

2. Put the walnut and olive oils into a screw-top jar. Add the pomegranate molasses and vinegar and shake well until combined.

3. Drizzle over the salad and sprinkle with toasted almonds and crushed peppercorns.

VEGETABLE SALAD WITH EGG

Serves 4
Preparation and cooking 20 minutes

Ingredients:

1 red capsicum (pepper), seeds removed and chopped

1 yellow capsicum (pepper), seeds removed and chopped

4 baby carrots, chopped

4 large tomatoes, seeds removed and chopped

4 spring (green) onions, finely chopped

2 tbsp cider vinegar

3 tbsp sunflower oil

sea salt

2 tbsp chopped mint

2 tbsp chopped parsley

2 tbsp chopped coriander (cilantro)

4 eggs

4 sprigs coriander, to garnish

Method:

1. Mix the vegetables together in a large bowl.

2. Mix the vinegar and oil, season with a little sea salt and stir into the vegetables. Set the salad aside.

3. Place the eggs in a pan of boiling water and boil for about 5 minutes. Cool the eggs under cold running water then carefully peel off the shells.

4. Stir the herbs into the salad and place in serving bowls. Add an egg to each bowl and garnish with a sprig of coriander (cilantro).

SUMMER VEGETABLE SPAGHETTI

Serves 4
Preparation and cooking 30 minutes

Ingredients:

4 medium zucchinis (courgettes)
2 avocados
2 limes, juice
5 tomatoes, deseeded and finely diced
2 sprigs dill (dill weed), tips finely chopped
4 tbsp sesame oil
3 tbsp cider vinegar
2 tbsp fish sauce
freshly ground black pepper
chilli powder
4 tbsp black sesame seeds
lime wedges, to serve

Method:

1. Cut the zucchinis (courgettes) into fine spaghetti strips using a spiral cutter or grater. Dice the avocado and drizzle immediately with lime juice.

2. Mix together the zucchini spaghetti, avocados, tomatoes and dill (dill weed). Mix the oil, vinegar and fish sauce through the vegetables and season to taste with ground black pepper and a pinch of chilli powder.

3. Arrange the mixture on plates and sprinkle with sesame seeds. Garnish with lime wedges and serve.

SUMMER SALAD

Serves 4
Preparation and cooking 20 minutes + soaking 24 hours + draining 24 hours

Ingredients:

For the salad:
2 handfuls lamb's lettuce (corn salad)
2 handfuls watercress
1 handful broad beans, blanched and skinned
1 large carrot, peeled and cut into thin strips
1 handful pink cress or red beetroot leaves
2 spring (green) onions, chopped
1 small bunch chervil or flat-leaf parsley, sprigged
1 bunch radishes, thinly sliced
12 cherries
6 tbsp Paleo cream cheese (see right and below)

For the dressing:
5 tbsp walnut oil
3 tbsp lemon juice
sea salt

For the Paleo cream cheese:
210 g | 7½ oz | 1½ cups cashew nuts
125 ml | 4½ fl oz | ½ cup cider vinegar
2 tbsp lemon juice
2 tbsp water
sea salt
black pepper

Method:

1. For the salad: mix together the lamb's lettuce (corn salad), watercress and broad beans and place in serving bowls.

2. Scatter over the remaining ingredients.

3. For the Paleo cream cheese: place the cashew nuts in a glass container, cover with water and leave to soak in the fridge for 24 hours. Drain well then rinse the nuts under cold water.

4. Place the soaked nuts in a blender with the remaining ingredients and blend for about two minutes or until you have a very smooth paste. Add a little more water if necessary.

5. Drape a piece of cheesecloth over the top of a tall container and scoop the cheese mixture into it. Pull the edges of the cheesecloth together to make a bundle and tie with a piece of string. Hang the bag of cheese from the handle of a wooden spoon and let it hang over the container to drain for 24 hours. Season the cheese with a little sea salt and black pepper if desired.

6. Mix together the walnut oil and lemon juice to make the dressing, season with a little sea salt and serve with crumbled Paleo cream cheese.

SIRLOIN STEAK WITH MEDITERRANEAN VEGETABLES

Serves 4
Preparation and cooking 35 minutes

Ingredients:

1 eggplant (aubergine), very thinly sliced

2 small zucchinis (courgettes), thinly sliced lengthways

2 capsicums (peppers), yellow and red, seeds removed, cut into strips

1 red onion, cut into wedges

6 tomatoes, halved or quartered if large

3 tbsp olive oil

2 tbsp balsamic vinegar

sea salt

freshly ground black pepper

2 cloves garlic, sliced

4 sirloin steaks

To garnish:
basil

Method:

1. Heat the grill.

2. Put all the vegetables into a bowl.

3. Mix together the olive oil, vinegar, salt, pepper and garlic. Pour over the vegetables and toss well to coat. Drain off the marinade and reserve.

4. Place the vegetables in the grill pan and grill for about 10 minutes, turning once, until tender.

5. Brush the steaks with the reserved marinade. Grill for 3–5 minutes on each side, until cooked to your liking.

6. Cut the steaks into thick slices and place on warm serving plates with the vegetables. Garnish with basil. If desired, serve with tomato salsa as a side dish.

Tip: A simple tomato salsa consists of 2 diced tomatoes, 2 tsp chopped coriander and half a diced red onion, combined and seasoned with sea salt.

DINNER

Try these recipes for healthy dinners that are
full of colour, flavour and nutritious ingredients.
They are easy to prepare for everyday dinners but
impressive enough for entertaining.

LAMB AND COCONUT CURRY

Serves 4
Preparation and cooking 2 hours

Ingredients:

2 tbsp olive oil
800 g | 28 oz lamb shoulder, diced
1 onion, chopped
3 cloves garlic, finely chopped
1 tbsp grated ginger (gingerroot)
1 red chilli, seeds removed, finely chopped
1 tsp turmeric
10 curry leaves
3–4 tbsp curry paste or powder
400 g | 14 oz | 2 cups canned chopped tomatoes
500 ml | 18 fl oz | 2 cups lamb stock (broth)
125 ml | 4½ fl oz | ½ cup coconut cream
1 ripe mango, peeled and chopped

To garnish:
coriander seeds, crushed
toasted desiccated (fine) coconut

Method:

1. Heat 1 tablespoon of oil in a flameproof casserole dish and brown the lamb for 3–4 minutes in batches. Remove with a slotted spoon, then set aside.

2. Add the remaining oil to the pan and cook the onion, stirring, for 2–3 minutes until softened. Add the garlic, ginger (gingerroot), chilli, turmeric and curry leaves and cook for 1 minute until fragrant.

3. Add the curry paste or powder, stir well to combine, then return the lamb to the pan, stirring to coat in the mixture.

4. Add the tomatoes and stock (broth), bring to a boil, then reduce the heat and simmer, uncovered, for about 90 minutes, until the lamb is tender.

5. Stir in the coconut cream and mango. Cook for a further 10 minutes, until the sauce has thickened.

6. Sprinkle with crushed coriander seeds and toasted coconut.

SALMON FILLET AND PRAWNS WITH VEGETABLES

Serves 4
Preparation and cooking 45 minutes

Ingredients:

1 onion, thickly sliced
2 bulbs fennel, thickly sliced
12 cherry tomatoes
2 figs, quartered
4 tbsp olive oil
salt
freshly ground pepper
4 salmon fillets
4 prawns (shrimp), peeled and deveined, tails on

To garnish:
lemon wedges
sage leaves

Method:

1. Heat the oven to 200°C (180°C fan | 400°F | gas 6).

2. Place the onion, fennel, cherry tomatoes and figs in a bowl, drizzle with 3 tablespoons olive oil and season with a grinding of salt and pepper. Toss well.

3. Spread out in a baking dish and cook for 15–20 minutes until almost tender.

4. Combine the remaining tablespoon of oil with a seasoning of salt and pepper. Brush over the top and sides of the salmon. Place skin-side down on top of the vegetables. Bake for 10–15 minutes, until the fish is opaque and flakes easily with a fork. Add the prawns (shrimp) for the last 8–10 minutes of cooking time, until they turn pink.

5. Garnish with lemon wedges and sage leaves.

ROLLED ROAST PORK

Serves 4–6
Preparation and cooking 2 hours

Ingredients:

1½–2 kg | 3⅓–4½ lb boneless pork loin
sea salt

For the stuffing:
2 tbsp olive oil
1 onion, finely chopped
2 cloves garlic, crushed
1 large cooking apple, peeled, cored and roughly chopped
140 g | 5 oz | 1 cup pistachios, roughly chopped
1 pomegranate, seeds only
handful of thyme and sage leaves, finely chopped
sea salt
freshly ground black pepper

Method:

1. Heat the oven to 230°C (210°C fan | 450°F | gas 8).

2. Place the pork loin skin-side up on a work surface. Using a very sharp knife, score the skin widthways at 1 cm | ½" intervals. Crumble sea salt all over the scored skin, rubbing it well into the cuts. Pat the salt all over the skin, then turn the meat over so the flesh side faces up.

3. For the stuffing: heat half the oil in a pan, add the onion and garlic and cook for 5–7 minutes, until slightly softened. Remove from the heat and allow to cool.

4. Mix together the apple, pistachios, pomegranate seeds, herbs and remaining oil in a bowl. Add the cooled onion mixture and mix well. Season well with sea salt and ground black pepper.

5. Place the stuffing down the centre of the pork then roll the meat up to form a thick cylinder. Tie with kitchen string down its length to secure the stuffing.

6. Put into a roasting tin. Roast for 25 minutes.

7. Reduce the oven temperature to 200°C (180°C fan | 400°F | gas 6). Roast for a further 60 minutes, until cooked through. The pork is cooked if the juices run clear when the thickest part of the flesh is pierced with a skewer.

8. Allow the meat to rest for 15 minutes before carving. Serve with Summer Salad (page 37) or a garden salad.

MEATBALLS IN TOMATO SAUCE

Serves 4
Preparation and cooking 1 hour

Ingredients:

For the meatballs:
450 g | 16 oz minced (ground) beef
1 tsp ground cumin
1 onion, grated
1 egg
salt
freshly ground black pepper
2 tbsp olive oil

For the tomato sauce:
1 kg | 2¼ lb ripe tomatoes
2 tbsp olive oil
1 onion, chopped
1 clove garlic, crushed
200 ml | 7 fl oz | ⅞ cup red wine or vegetable stock (broth)
salt and pepper

To garnish:
basil
capers, rinsed

Method:

1. For the meatballs: mix together all the ingredients (except the oil) until well blended. Form the mixture into about 20 balls.

2. Heat the oil in a frying pan (skillet) over a medium heat and fry the meatballs in batches until browned on all sides. Remove from the pan and set aside.

3. For the tomato sauce: put the tomatoes into boiling water for a few seconds, then skin, halve, remove the seeds and chop the tomatoes.

4. Heat the oil in a frying pan and cook the onion and garlic for a few minutes until soft. Add the tomatoes and wine or stock (broth), reduce the heat and simmer gently for about 15 minutes until thickened. Season to taste with salt and pepper.

5. Add the meatballs to the pan. Cover them in the sauce and cook for 5–10 minutes until cooked through.

6. Garnish with basil and capers.

FISHERMAN'S STEW

Serves 4
Preparation and cooking 40 minutes

Ingredients:

1 tbsp olive oil
1 large sweet potato (yam), cubed
½ onion, chopped
3–5 cloves garlic
1 dried red chilli, finely chopped
425 ml | 15 fl oz | 1¾ cups fish stock (broth)
400 g | 14 oz | 2 cups canned chopped tomatoes
15–20 clams
225 g | 8 oz scallops, cut if large
250 g | 9 oz squid, cut into rings
300 g | 11 oz firm white fish fillets, cubed
salt
freshly ground black pepper

To garnish:
chopped flat-leaf parsley

Method:

1. Heat the olive oil in a large pan over a medium heat. Add the sweet potato (yam) and cook for about 5 minutes until softened. Add the onion and garlic, season and cook for a further 5 minutes until softened.

2. Add the chilli, stock (broth) and tomatoes and cook for 5 minutes.

3. Bring to a boil, then reduce the heat and simmer for 10 minutes.

4. Add the clams, scallops, squid and fish fillets. Cover and cook for about 5 minutes until the seafood is cooked. Season to taste with salt and pepper.

5. Ladle into warm serving bowls and sprinkle with parsley.

CHILLI CHICKEN WITH SALAD

Serves 4
Preparation and cooking 1 hour 15 minutes

Ingredients:

For the chicken:
8 free-range chicken drumsticks
4 tbsp coconut oil
1 onion, finely chopped
2 cloves garlic, finely chopped
2 tsp chilli powder, or more, according to taste
1 tsp ground cumin
4 large tomatoes, seeds removed and chopped
1 tbsp chopped thyme
2 tbsp cider vinegar
2 tbsp honey
kernels from 1 corn cob
sea salt

For the salad:
2 handfuls baby spinach, washed
1 small red onion, sliced
½ cucumber, finely sliced
1 small mango, peeled and sliced
2 tbsp chopped parsley
juice of one lemon
3 tbsp walnut oil
4 slices lime

Method:

1. Make two slashes in each of the chicken drumsticks with a sharp knife. Heat half the oil in a wide, deep pan and sear the drumsticks over a high heat until they are lightly browned – you may have to do this in batches. Remove the drumsticks from the pan and set aside.

2. Heat the remaining oil in the pan and gently cook the onion until soft but not brown. Add the garlic, cook for two minutes then add the chilli powder and cumin and cook for one more minute, stirring all the time.

3. Add the tomatoes, thyme, vinegar and honey, bring to a simmer then return the chicken to the pan. Cook very gently for 30–40 minutes, stirring from time to time, or until the chicken is tender. Add the corn kernels and season to taste with a little sea salt.

4. For the salad, mix the leaves, onion, cucumber and mango together, scatter over the parsley and dress with the lemon juice and walnut oil. Add a slice of lime to each salad.

PORK BELLY STEW

Serves 4–6
Preparation and cooking 4 hours 15 minutes

Ingredients:

1⅓ kg | 3 lb piece belly pork
1 onion, chopped
4 carrots, sliced
2 sticks celery, chopped
2 leeks, chopped
2 sweet potatoes (yams), sliced
2 cooking apples, chopped
2 sprigs thyme
1 l | 35 fl oz | 4 cups vegetable stock (broth), more if needed
salt
freshly ground pepper

To garnish:
flat-leaf parsley

Method:

1. Put the pork into a large heavy-based pan. Add the vegetables, apples and thyme and pour in the stock (broth). The pork should be just covered with liquid.

2. Bring to a boil and skim off any froth. Reduce the heat to a simmer, cover and simmer for 3–3 ½ hours until the pork is tender.

3. Heat the oven to 200°C (180°C fan | 400°F | gas 6).

4. Remove the pork from the pan and place fat-side up in a roasting tin. Add some of the liquid from the pan to the bottom of the tin.

5. Sprinkle the pork with salt and pepper and cook for 20–30 minutes until the fat is crisp and golden.

6. Remove the pork from the oven and allow to cool slightly before cutting into chunks.

7. Put the pork into warm serving bowls and ladle the contents of the pan into the bowls. Sprinkle with parsley.

COCONUT-COATED PRAWNS

Serves 4
Preparation and cooking 50 minutes

Ingredients:

20 large prawns (shrimps), shelled, tail on
100 g | 3½ oz | 1 cup coconut flour
1 tsp sea salt
1 tsp paprika
3 egg whites, lightly beaten
250 g | 9 oz | 2½ cups coconut flakes
lime wedges, to serve

Method:

1. Heat the oven to 200°C (180°C fan | 400°F | gas 6). Grease a baking tray (sheet) with a little oil.

2. Wash the prawns (shrimps) and pat dry with kitchen paper. Season the coconut flour with the sea salt and paprika and place in a flat dish.

3. Dredge the prawns through the seasoned flour, shake off any excess then dip into the egg whites and then into the coconut flakes, ensuring each prawn is well coated.

4. Place the prawns on the baking tray and bake in the oven for 15–20 minutes, turning once. Serve with the lime wedges alongside.

DESSERT

Following a Paleo diet doesn't mean you have to deny yourself dessert. These delicious dessert recipes use ingredients such as fresh fruits, nuts and honey so you can still enjoy some sweetness in your life.

LEMON CAKE WITH PINE NUTS

Makes 1 cake
Preparation and cooking 1 hour

Ingredients:

185 g | 6½ oz | 2 cups almond flour
65 g | 2¼ oz | ½ cup coconut flour
½ tsp salt
1 tsp bicarbonate of (baking) soda
230 g | 8 oz | ⅔ cup honey, warmed
150 ml | 5 fl oz | ⅔ cup coconut oil, melted
4 eggs
155 ml | 5½ fl oz | ⅔ cup coconut milk
2 tbsp lemon juice
1 tbsp grated lemon zest
100 g | 3½ oz | 1 cup pine nuts

Method:

1. Heat the oven to 180°C (160°C fan | 350°F | gas 4). Grease a 20 cm | 8" deep loose-based cake tin and line the base with non-stick baking paper.

2. Sift the dry ingredients into a mixing bowl and stir to combine.

3. Whisk together the honey and oil, then add the eggs, one at a time, whisking after each addition.

4. Add the coconut milk, lemon juice and zest, and beat until well combined.

5. Make a well in the centre of the dry ingredients and pour in the wet ingredients. Stir thoroughly until smooth.

6. Put mixture into the tin and sprinkle the pine nuts on top.

7. Bake for about 35 minutes until golden and springy to the touch. Cool in the tin for 10 minutes, then place on a wire rack to cool completely.

COCONUT ICE-CREAM WITH POMEGRANATE SEEDS

Serves 4
Preparation and cooking 30 minutes + 7 hours freezing

Ingredients:

450 ml | 16 fl oz | 2 cups coconut milk
3 egg yolks
50 g | 1¾ oz | ⅛ cup honey, warmed
50 ml | 1¾ fl oz | ⅕ cup coconut oil
few drops vanilla extract
75 g | 2 ½ oz | 1 cup desiccated (fine) coconut

To decorate:
pomegranate seeds

Method:

1. Heat the milk in a pan until almost boiling. Do not boil.

2. Whisk together the egg yolks and honey until thick, then whisk in the hot coconut milk with the coconut oil.

3. Return to the pan and cook very gently, stirring constantly until thickened. Do not boil.

4. Remove from the heat, add the vanilla and coconut and leave to cool, stirring occasionally.

5. If you have an ice-cream machine, churn according to the manufacturer's instructions, and continue to step 7.

6. Alternatively, pour into a freezerproof container and freeze for 4 hours, beating with a fork 2–3 times to break up the ice crystals.

7. Freeze for 2–3 hours until firm. Place in the refrigerator about 30 minutes before serving.

8. Scoop into chilled glasses with the pomegranate seeds.

CHOCOLATE FRUIT SLICE

Serves 4
Preparation and cooking 1 hour 30 minutes

Ingredients:

250 g | 9 oz sugar-free dairy-free dark (semisweet) chocolate, roughly chopped
3 tbsp honey
150 g | 5 oz | 1 cup almonds, roughly chopped
200 g | 7 oz | 1 cup dried apricots, roughly chopped
120 g | 4 oz | 1 cup dried cranberries

Method:

1. Melt the chopped chocolate in a bowl over a pan of gently simmering water, taking care that the bottom of the bowl doesn't touch the water.

2. Remove the bowl from the pan and stir in the honey.

3. Reserve about a quarter of the almonds, apricots and cranberries and mix the rest into the chocolate.

4. Spread the chocolate mixture onto a baking tray (sheet) lined with greaseproof paper and scatter over the reserved fruit and nuts.

5. Chill in the fridge for at least one hour or until the chocolate is set. Store in an airtight container for up to two weeks.

WATERMELON SORBET WITH CHOCOLATE AND NUTS

Serves 6
Preparation and cooking 30 minutes + 4 hours freezing

Ingredients:

1 watermelon, 1¾ kg | 3¾ lb approx; quartered, seeds removed
2 limes, juice
2 tbsp honey, warmed
100 g | 3½ oz | 1 cup chopped pistachio nuts
110 g | 4 oz | ¾ cup dairy-free sugar-free chocolate chips

Method:

1. Scoop the melon flesh into a food processor and blend until smooth.

2. Strain into a bowl and stir in the lime juice and honey, mixing well.

3. Place the mixture in a freezerproof loaf-shaped container and freeze for 2 hours. Mash finely with a fork and return to the freezer.

4. Freeze for a further 2 hours, mashing well every 30 minutes. Add the pistachios and chocolate chips after the final mashing and serve.

BANANA SOUFFLÉS

Serves 4
Preparation and cooking 40 minutes

Ingredients:

4 eggs, separated
¼ tsp salt
150 g | 5 oz | 7 tbsp runny honey
60 ml | 2 fl oz | ¼ cup coconut oil, melted
300 g | 11 oz | 1 cup mashed very ripe bananas
1 tsp vanilla extract

Method:

1. Heat the oven to 180°C (160°C fan | 350°F | gas 4). Grease 4–6 ovenproof cups and place on a baking tray (sheet).

2. Whisk the egg whites until stiff.

3. Whisk together the remaining ingredients until blended. Gently fold into the egg whites until no white streaks remain.

4. Pour into the cups and bake for 15–20 minutes until golden and risen. Serve immediately.

BISCOTTI WITH PISTACHIOS AND FIGS

Makes 20–24 biscotti
Preparation and cooking 1 hour 10 minutes + 20 minutes cooling

Ingredients:

120 g | 4 oz | ½ cup honey
2 eggs
2 tsp vanilla extract
285 g | 10 oz | 3 cups almond flour
¼ tsp salt
½ tsp bicarbonate of (baking) soda
75 g | 2½ oz | ½ cup chopped dried figs
100 g | 3½ oz | 1 cup chopped pistachio nuts

Method:

1. Heat the oven to 170°C (150°C fan | 335°F | gas 3). Line a large baking tray (sheet) with non-stick baking paper.

2. Whisk together the honey, eggs and vanilla in a mixing bowl until light and fluffy.

3. Stir together the almond flour, salt and bicarbonate of (baking) soda.

4. Add the dry ingredients to the wet and stir until combined, then fold in the figs and pistachios.

5. Turn out the dough onto non-stick baking paper and shape into a log about 30 cm | 12" long.

6. Place the log on the baking tray and flatten until about 7 cm | 3" wide.

7. Bake for 30 minutes, then leave to cool for 20 minutes.

8. Cut the log on an angle into 1 cm | ½" slices with a serrated knife. Space the biscuits slightly apart and bake for 10 minutes, then turn them over and bake for a further 10–15 minutes until dry and crisp. Turn off the oven and cool in the oven.

GINGER AND COCONUT MACAROONS

Makes 10 macaroons
Preparation and cooking 30 minutes

Ingredients:

2 egg whites
70 g | 2½ oz | 10 tsp honey
¼ tsp salt
2 tsp ground ginger
190 g | 7 oz | 2½ cups desiccated (fine) coconut
100 g | 3 ½ oz sugar-free dairy-free dark (semisweet) chocolate

Method:

1. Place the egg whites and honey in a bowl and whisk until frothy, but not stiff. Stir in the salt, ginger and coconut. Chill for 30 minutes.

2. Heat the oven to 180°C (160°C fan | 350°F | gas 4). Line 2 baking trays (sheets) with non-stick baking paper.

3. Drop the mixture in small heaps onto the trays. Bake for about 10–15 minutes until firm and tinged golden brown. Leave to cool on the trays.

4. Melt the chocolate in a heatproof bowl over a pan of simmering (not boiling) water. Remove from the heat and set aside to cool and thicken.

5. Spoon the chocolate over the macaroons and leave to set.

CHOCOLATE ALMOND CAKE WITH BLUEBERRIES

Makes 1 cake
Preparation and cooking 1 hour

Ingredients:

240 g | 8 oz | 1 cup almond butter
85 ml | 3 fl oz | ⅜ cup maple syrup
1 egg, lightly beaten
2 tbsp coconut oil
65 g | 2¼ oz | ½ cup cocoa powder
½ tsp bicarbonate of (baking) soda
150 g | 5 oz | 1 cup almonds, roughly chopped
cocoa powder, for dredging

To serve:
blueberries

Method:

1. Heat the oven to 160°C (140°C fan | 325°F | gas 3). Grease and line a 25 cm | 9" square baking tin.

2. Beat together the almond butter, maple syrup, egg and coconut oil in a large bowl.

3. Fold in the cocoa powder and bicarbonate of (baking) soda. Set aside a few of the chopped almonds then fold the rest into the cake mixture.

4. Pour the batter into the prepared tin and bake in the oven for 20–25 minutes.

5. Let the cake cool in the tin then scatter over the reserved almonds and cut into 12 pieces. Dredge a little cocoa powder over the top and serve with the blueberries.

DRINKS

These drink recipes range from refreshing spritzers and punches to fresh fruit juices and smoothies. There's even a recipe for an indulgent Paleo Spiced Hot Chocolate.

ORANGE AND POMEGRANATE JUICE

Serves 4
Preparation and cooking 10 minutes

Ingredients:

1 pomegranate, seeds
crushed ice
250 ml | 9 fl oz | 1 cup pomegranate juice
4 oranges, juice

Method:

1. Place the pomegranate seeds in the bottom of 4 glasses.

2. Fill each glass with crushed ice and pour over the pomegranate juice.

3. Add the orange juice and serve immediately.

SPICED HOT CHOCOLATE

Serves 4
Preparation and cooking 15 minutes

Ingredients:

675 ml | 24 fl oz | 3 cups coconut or almond milk
25 g | 1 oz | ¼ cup cacao powder
1 tsp vanilla extract
¼ tsp ground cardamom
1 tsp ground cinnamon
1 pinch grated nutmeg
1 star anise
100 g | 3½ oz sugar-free dairy-free dark (semisweet) chocolate, chopped
honey, to taste
4 cinnamon sticks

Method:

1. Heat the coconut milk, cacao powder, vanilla, cardamom, ground cinnamon, nutmeg and star anise in a pan until hot.

2. Bring to a simmer and stir in the chopped chocolate. Simmer, stirring for 1–2 minutes, then add honey to taste.

3. Remove the star anise, pour into cups and add a cinnamon stick to each cup.

WATERMELON AND LIME JUICE

Serves 4–6
Preparation and cooking 10 minutes

Ingredients:

1⅔ kg | 3⅔ lb watermelon flesh, seeds removed
4 limes, juice
2 tbsp honey, warmed
lime slices
ice

Method:

1. Put the watermelon flesh, lime juice and honey in a blender or food processor and blend until smooth.

2. Pour into a jug and add the lime slices. Chill well before serving.

3. Fill the glasses with ice before pouring the drink.

BLACKBERRY SPRITZERS

Serves 4
Preparation and cooking 20 minutes

Ingredients:

200 g | 7 oz | 2 cups blackberries
1 lemon, juice
500–700 ml | 18–25 fl oz | 2–3 cups sparkling water
2–4 tbsp runny honey
ice

To decorate:
mint leaves
blackberries

Method:

1. Puree the blackberries in a blender or food processor. Push the blackberry puree through a sieve to remove the seeds.

2. Combine the blackberry puree, lemon juice, sparkling water and honey to taste.

3. Fill 4 glasses with ice. Pour the blackberry mixture over the ice and decorate with mint leaves and blackberries.

MANDARIN PUNCH

Serves 6-8
Preparation and cooking 10 minutes

Ingredients:

375 ml | 13 fl oz | 1½ cups mandarin juice
250 ml | 9 fl oz | 1 cup apple juice
30 ml | 1 fl oz | ⅛ cup lemon juice
750 ml | 26 fl oz | 3 cups sparkling water

Method:

1. Mix together all the ingredients and chill before serving.

HEALTHY GREEN SMOOTHIES

Serves 4
Preparation and cooking 10 minutes + 1 hour chilling

Ingredients:

4 handfuls baby spinach, washed and roughly chopped
6 kiwi fruit, peeled and roughly chopped
4 tsp wheatgrass powder
750 ml | 26 fl oz | 3 cups coconut water
2 limes, juice

Method:

1. Place all the ingredients in a blender and blend until smooth.

2. Chill in the fridge for one hour then pour into four glasses and serve.

RASPBERRY ORANGE ICED TEA

Serves 4
Preparation and cooking 15 minutes

Ingredients:

4 tsp herb tea leaves
900 ml | 32 fl oz | 4 cups boiling water
honey, to taste
2 oranges, juice
½ lemon, juice

To decorate:
ice
1 unwaxed orange, thinly sliced
raspberries

Method:

1. Add the tea leaves to the boiling water and pour into a teapot. Leave to stand for 15–20 minutes.

2. Strain into a jug and stir in the honey until dissolved.

3. Stir in the orange and lemon juices and chill before serving.

4. Divide the ice and orange slices between chilled glasses and pour in the tea. Decorate with raspberries.

Tip: Any caffeine-free herbal teas would suit this recipe, e.g. rose petal/bud, camomile, lemongrass.

SUMMER BERRY SMOOTHIES

Serves 4
Preparation and cooking 10 minutes

Ingredients:

100 ml | 3 ½ fl oz | 7 tbsp orange juice
225 ml | 8 fl oz | 1 cup almond or coconut milk
50 g | 1¾ oz | ½ cup blueberries
65 g | 2¼ oz | ½ cup raspberries or strawberries
1 ripe banana

Method:

1. Put all the ingredients in a blender or food processor and blend until smooth.

2. Pour into chilled glasses and serve immediately.

WEIGHTS AND MEASURES

Weights and measures differ from country to country, but with these handy conversion charts cooking has never been easier!

Weight Measures

Metric	Imperial
10 g	¼ oz
15 g	½ oz
20 g	¾ oz
30 g	1 oz
60 g	2 oz
115 g	4 oz (¼ lb)
125 g	4½ oz
145 g	5 oz
170 g	6 oz
185 g	6½ oz
200 g	7 oz
225 g	8 oz (½ lb)
300 g	10½ oz
330 g	11½ oz
370 g	13 oz
400 g	14 oz
425 g	15 oz
455 g	16 oz (1 lb)
500 g	17½ oz (1 lb 1½ oz)
600 g	21 oz (1 lb 5 oz)
650 g	23 oz (1 lb 7 oz)
750 g	26½ oz (1 lb 10½ oz)
1000 g (1 kg)	35 oz (2 lb 3 oz)

Cup Measurements

One cup of these commonly used Paleo ingredients is equal to the following weights.

Ingredient	Metric	Imperial
Almond butter	225 g	8 oz
Apples (dried and chopped)	125 g	4½ oz
Apricots (dried and chopped)	190 g	6¾ oz
Coconut (desiccated/fine)	90 g	3 oz
Coconut flour	115 g	4 oz
Fruit (dried)	170 g	6 oz
Honey	315 g	11 oz
Nuts (chopped)	115 g	4 oz
Sugar-free dairy-free choc bits	155 g	5½ oz

Liquid Measures

Cup	Metric	Imperial
¼ cup	63 ml	2¼ fl oz
½ cup	125 ml	4½ fl oz
¾ cup	188 ml	6⅔ fl oz
1 cup	250 ml	8¾ fl oz
1¾ cup	438 ml	15½ fl oz
2 cups	500 ml	17½ fl oz
4 cups	1 litre	35 fl oz

Spoon	Metric	Imperial
¼ teaspoon	1.25 ml	1/25 fl oz
½ teaspoon	2.5 ml	1/12 fl oz
1 teaspoon	5 ml	⅙ fl oz
1 tablespoon	15 ml	½ fl oz

Oven Temperatures

Celsius	Fahrenheit	Gas mark
120	250	1
150	300	2
160	320	3
180	350	4
190	375	5
200	400	6
220	430	7
230	450	8
250	480	9

INDEX

Almond and Carrot Bread	18
Banana Soufflés	69
Belgian Waffles	17
Biscotti with Pistachios and Figs	70
Blackberry Spritzers	85
Carrot and Cinnamon Muffins	9
Chilli Chicken with Salad	53
Chilli Chicken Wraps	25
Chocolate Almond Cake with Blueberries	74
Chocolate Fruit Slice	65
Coconut-Coated Prawns	57
Coconut Ice-Cream with Pomegranate Seeds	62
Fisherman's Stew	50
Fluffy Baked Eggs with Roasted-Vegetable Hash	21
Fritters with Mushroom Sauce	13
Ginger and Coconut Macaroons	73
Healthy Green Smoothies	89
Lamb and Coconut Curry	42
Lemon Cake with Pine Nuts	61
Mandarin Punch	86
Meatballs in Tomato Sauce	49
Mussels in Curry Broth	29
Nut and Seed Breakfast	14
Orange and Pomegranate Juice	78
Pancakes with Bananas	6
Pork Belly Stew	54
Raspberry Orange Iced Tea	90
Rolled Roast Pork	46
Salmon Fillet and Prawns with Vegetables	45
Sirloin Steak with Mediterranean Vegetables	38
Smoked Duck Salad	30
Spiced Hot Chocolate	81
Spicy Sweet-Potato Soup	26
Summer Berry Smoothies	93
Summer Salad	37
Summer Vegetable Spaghetti	34
Vegetable Frittatas	10
Vegetable Salad with Egg	33
Watermelon and Lime Juice	82
Watermelon Sorbet with Chocolate and Nuts	66